MW00903031

LINGER, STILL

Linger, Still

AISLINN HUNTER

GASPEREAU PRESS ❧ PRINTERS & PUBLISHERS   MMXVII

for G.

for the animals

Go now.
    Beside the uncertainties

in black veils
    stand the certainties.

—DERMOT HEALY

the body breaks into pixels, machine failure—
aches, pains, a dimming.

What once thrummed
now flashes *Error*—

so that whatever philosophy
you sailed in on,

whatever two-minute film of
'a day on the beach in June' that said

this was my life to you,
comes stuttering to a halt.

Then, a silence, a proclivity
to witness,

an anonymity that wants nothing
but to linger.

In this last lick of light
before the day gives out, listen:

there are masterworks painted
by the wholly forgotten and unnamed,

and there are Rembrandts and Bruegels
so wasted and decayed

no semblance of art history
can remake them.

That is us: the dust in the room
where the new paintings hang—

but oh, the music
in that sweeping.

And so, one day, the world begins.
A vastness so eternal, there are not enough letters, or words, or days to name it.
When we speak, it becomes small: the speck of our concentration.

Little fish brains, hearts slick as minnows.
How some animals express more with the flick of a tail.

Seeing this, the Greeks invented optimism—
but when it worked like an aqueduct trundling water to distant cities
they lowered buckets of grief into the largest wells.

Drinking it, Alcibiades asked: What use is my land
if the plaque of the world bears no trace of me?

The earth, according to Socrates, a platter of good and bad food:
crusted bread, green-tipped figs, honey from Mt Hymettus laced with thyme.
A pear with worm in it.

I prefer Thales who saw the earth as a slab of wood floating on water.
Days I am that bereft, days I drift and splinter.

This was before people wanted their lives *said*.
Winter—a world of change, fluid but plain.

Here, the economy of the dogs' bony ribs, bare
trees and thin-necked birds that lean into the season.

In the valley the villagers' shadows boxed behind them like coffins.
A cyclical world: the cut across, the turn at the end.

Rabbits so far down their burrows it's as if we dreamed them.
Even the ravens sweep their wings overhead, and then leave.

Three men trudging home, the blood tracks of game
stitching the snow red behind them.

If you are looking for meaning you won't find it here.
In the village dogs let loose their howls, ice cracks—

the world a shuttered window unconcerned with
the muted beauty of a lace curtain against frosted glass.

Nothing stays: the rafters go in, the rafters sag, and time
polishes his pocket watch on a shroud of snow.

Once unfurls into *and then*. The wind moves around
the story with no centre. The men set out again, and again.

A century picks up its sails and passes.
The currents less predictable the farther out we get.

↓ Oh, heart—

acclimate the house to dusk—
        pulleys and levers of blinds, sigh of light switch,
toggle it all toward evening

that I can make it dim at 11a.m., close myself in,
        even advent autumn—
sling back the red tongue of the thermostat, that hound
thirsty for water, the real summer, obdurate sun, a pauper
clanging her tin cup behind the curtains

slack in its giving, hale fellow contingency—
        mood-setter, party planner
turned toward me one minute, then gawping off the next
like the chair I fall into

        swivel of self, again, again, and again
too much everything

a garbage bag billows out the neighbour's window—
        mid-afternoon, near-suburbia,
even the TV trophied out and nothing seen

how blaring the sidewalk that it fascinates us so, how eye-clad
        this phone, how speaks my truth to it
that it might portal me Walden when I like—
picture-click the lake chromatic under the sun's
bright stamp of approval

maybe this window's bucking hollow is why I distrust
        the man hawking pamphlets,
the dogless woman who carries Milk-Bones in her pockets,
landscapes I would reshape were I not voyaging only as far as the market

        oh milk, oh lemons, oh cod, how coyly
you opal the counter; lock-pick the heart

all day construction next door—nail guns firing,
        the cement truck beeping backwards,
a wood chipper clot-mouthed and full of spite

a barrage as incessant as the news—airport bombs, black men shot,
        a truck driven through a crowd on a street I've walked down—
everywhere people unhinging, twitter lit up with #missing
#pleasehelpfind mywife/myhusband/mypartner/
myfather/mother/brother/sister/friend/child

the world on loudspeaker while I drink from a blue
        ceramic mug with a skull pegged at the bottom—
death rising from the pool of my coffee, death
nodding me to sleep in my tea

        a vacuum I satellite my self around—
black hole, dark matter

in *What is Art?* Tolstoy suggests that
        to contemplate is to reveal—
and so we have painted tax gatherers, ambassadors

a boy posed as Bacchus, a man with a pansy and a skull—
        such surrogate weepings
and have made an art of aura, that Romantic theory of reflection
easily seen in old photos at the vintage shop—
here, a lady in an ostrich hat, there, a man juggling oranges

a truth in every image—the Polaroid of the twins in leg warmers,
        the woman on the news showing her scars,
the girl I was in my communion gown,
the father leaning over the side of the boat

        what lists under every pose: the hope
that someone will love us

of effort there's not much to be said—
>	upswing, downswing, surge of hope, a wavering that's
a yard of planters still burdened with last year's dirt

unsemestered at last, I barrel woodward,
>	huff past trees limned in a hallelujah morning
Kantian in its aesthetics—even the border collies
are more beautiful here, nosing left then right at the fork,
hurtling toward the river

some woods you get lost in, some, lose you—*thin difference*, I say—
>	under the intangible there's always an ache—
the BBC webcasting the countryside with unfailing optimism,
the jubilance of 'Now, let's go live to the wrens!'

>	oh little gargoyles, oh feathering imps—
how I run toward the possibility of your survival

what little space one needs, a revelation
        paired to the season—how fair,
how unscreened, how habitable the outdoors

my concerns so small I can marvel at the bell
        someone's tied to a tree—
chime of hello, debutante of the dogwood, clamour
of the hours unfolding against Plato's warning
that we not fall for the passing show

again, this suspicion that I'm the sloe-eyed, sandal-shuffler
        in Socrates' arguments, the false know-it-all—
and envy? yes—it's that girl in the park, dressed prep school,
her father's arm around her shoulders

        that I was not like that, had no ease about me,
that my skirts did not have such pleats

because of the want that nothing be raw,
        that my rightness grace the tables of others, I will
myself glad-laced, thoughts a pool of honey

and drift hallways in the great house of memory,
        and wake the boy asleep in the barn with my crying—
a boy I demand the pastoral of, who I beg tell me
what the shutters see in their long nights
staring at the moon

such obvious transgressions—how I city-mouth the countryside,
        picnic on its vocabulary,
unspool strawberries from others' gardens,
make pure the preserves

        even reference Shakespeare —you know the one—
so clever he'd often slap his own thigh

enter again disquiet—
  the havoc of traffic, car horns acclaiming the causeway,
tinted windows flipping off the rain

this one's mouth moving stereo, bass-thrum of a BMW's heartbeat,
  the gas station a welter of bad weather—
yes, hello, dear pump-neighbours,
how, like Pound, I wish your shiny faces would petal,
the day unblot your despair

remember when the world was a patch with a name on it?
  a jogging vitality that *good day*'d the frame
of your car window—the fuel gauges white-eyed and rolling back
like a child submitting to sleep

  oh digital now, forgive this ticking nostalgia,
our cloud-kissed faces drifting past the side-mirrors

the banks closed, long weekend gusty, short on rent again,
        we sit in traffic bedecking the road,
move in exhausted inches

and expound and arch Romantic, and risk ridiculousness—
        ode of billboard, elegy of sun,
how idle we flâneurs of the causeway—
this city a parking lot of highways and byways,
ornate bridges spiking the sky

these cash-strapped years, this city of accidents and jumpers
        a hope-clogged transport—
that straggle-haired woman in the Safeway? so tired—
though her face lit a Sunday school epiphany

        when she looked into the mirror above the radishes
and saw she was me

ferried, spluttering, we Jonah ourselves onto the pier—
        a graceless transport, our car and camper
freighting us over this blistered rock

oh age-spotted Earth, do not spite us, unmotor us back to the Greeks,
        we are already mediaevaling ourselves—
sing a litany of rations, oracles of incalescence,
bear ash-borne Pompeian dreams—
survival boxes in every basement we yacht past

how late the day, the woman automating frozen dinners
        across the scanner seems to say, *how overripe the season,*
her lipstick blooming under halogen, decades away from the
candy store concerns of childhood—that world where we could still run

        bright plastic animals girding our waists—
into the cooling pool

dirt-lit and back from camping
        we carry our gear from the car—
milk-soured Coleman, sprung sleeping bags, two clouds of pillow

until—you inside cracking a beer, the dogs lapping water—
        in the heft of a duffel I suddenly remember
a film clip of Jacqueline du Pré
lifting her cello from the boot of a Hillman,
the wind tugging her long blonde hair

how strange it is to find her here—
        a woman known for an elegy,
turning toward the camera and into her own beauty,
caught in the act of seeing herself seen

        oh macula of self, time's dust pixelling—
that was the year I was born

waist-pooled, full-chested, how arteried
       the body blooms its want—
unsleek, conspicuous, I girth my everywhere

and remember standing on a marbled floor before
       da Vinci's sketch of an ox heart,
my mouth cast against its exactness in the glass—
ventricle paths, filling chambers—a dissection perfected
on the budding grass of a hilltop farm

in those years we lived in a 17th century square, caught up in
       the pub swill of history, poring over each part,
even gracing your grandfather's rural village
with our gawp-eyed presence

       remember that blue trough of sky?
how long we stood there

the floor—wood plank, bereft of polish,
        stripped by years, the wear of former inhabitants—
welts of winter boots, snow sliding to puddle

this morning a friend's baby girl on that floor laughing
        at her upturned bowl of cereal—the dogs lapping it up
as if it's a kind of grace, like those daily offerings
that slip into the cracks and crevices, bow out dully:
nub of sock, strand of hair, plant leaves dropping like alms

what falls away when we come home through the door
        and out of what's expected of us—
oh, rough atomic self,
let's learn from this impermanence

        how even the breeze that comes in behind us takes,
light as a pickpocket, as much as it gives

yesterday we woke up, made love, slept til noon,
        revelling in laziness, straddling that fine
dotted line between indulgence and entitlement

but today, again, I'm waiting out the weather—
        warm front, cold front, storms in the troposphere,
that niggling fear that I sometimes love people just to see
if the wall in front of me will turn into a door—
the good weather temporary, the bad weather temporary

and in between, hours spent poring over books
        about the golden age, when whole
paintings were made to commemorate the gift of a pineapple...
repeat what you said about the rain

        is how the line in the Godard film goes—
repeat what you said about the rain

the house next door a monster: six bedrooms, four baths,
        a minotaur mazing his way to the property line
where he chainsaws our ivy through the slats of the fence

this, how we learn to live tight-lipped, wave like the queen,
        feel the world's sharp edges—
but still, there are cloudless days: sunroof open,
dogs in the backseat panting all the way to the swimming hole,
a walk in the woods with friends

afternoons where we arrive urban, order pizza, do patio,
        drink a good red on the bay—
maybe Arendt was right?
it's the things of the world that stabilize us

        light on the water, light in our eyes,
light refracting light

summer, brilliant, flags its way across the city—
        hymn of the car wash, queue of propane;
the population of lawn chairs booms

oh glorious outdoors! waft of barbeque, splutter of hot tub,
        how your martini shakers castanet the block!
how purvey your children their lemonade,
again, the dachshund running amok—*Ava! Ava! Ava!*
a street of sprinklers waving *hello, goodbye, hello*

the questions still the same: *how to be good, how to be,*
        let go of this parched trying;
the honeybees in the woods bursting out of their hive again—
oh, small buzzing testimony-makers, I hear you

        yes! let this be enough—
the honeycomb of the heart full of honey

 *I Came to See the Beautiful Things*

Start small. Wonder
if I should name them:
orders, genus, species—
wonder, too,
if I should make death's
dark similes beautiful—
how, eyeless, the birds appear
to be feigning sleep—
children squinting too much
to be convincing.

I did not expect death
or preservation, did not expect
stasis to smell the way it does—
tang of some unknown
ointment, sharp burst
of ethanol in which the body
was christened.

It's astonishing to me
in this world's traffic,
that this hummingbird,
posed in her
downward drift
toward the honeysuckle,
will last five hundred years.

When we are dust
on the dust of our
dead children's graves
she will still be here—
the petal of an improbable flower
a few inches from her beak—

its gold coin of pollen
glinting—
a fee for the ferryman
she can't reach.

A hundred slow curtsies
in filmy skirts
upends us, returns us,
briefly, to ourselves.
The jar held up to the window,
clutch of eggs swaying in the light.
A dance that goes back millennia,
that once saw
Simon Fraser's paddle
dip down through green
streaming chandeliers
on his way to a river
that would one day
forge his name.

Each egg a bathysphere—
a pip-sized possibility,
a helmet diver, scooped
with the stick it was moored on,
out of the wind-stirred stream.
How clear it is here
in the filigreed cloud of this
ancient bedding,
to see that being born is the rarity—
to see how the odds are stacked
against navigation—
to marvel at the possibility
of arrival, at how anything
becomes anything
at all.

Becomes fossil, what once patterned sound—
sound conveyed as if on a fine tray
along the jawbone
of a blue universe—

this one lugging Delphic hymns,
a freight of thought;
a trowel-headed trawler, deep
in love with her own singing.

Her *otolith*, the size of a human heart—
rust-red, elegantly lobed,
its *lub-dubh* lost
under Atlantic stereophonics—

ship engines, sonic pings,
mining hydraulics—oh, you
brawling symphonies—
plumes of heavy metal—

how you make a strike of stars
above and below, tectonic frictions—
the coral beds winking out,
ship's propellers glinting.

And so I say *Hail, deaf instrument*—
anchored
in your padded box in the after-
hours of this museum.

The air forced through the vents
is a poor approximation of wind—

though there are days I swear
it lifts my hair and sways

the soughing halls
of your skeleton.

CENTRAL AMERICAN SQUIRREL MONKEY, MALE SKELETON,
FROM THE SUFFIELD EXPERIMENTAL STATION, ALBERTA, 1951

How to do death better?

The squirrel monkey
has three kinds of call:
squeals, whistles, chirps.

A black cap, long red tail,
largest brain of any primate,
relative to body size.

Sprayed with sarin, one monkey
convulsed at six minutes
and died at twenty-nine.

What does that interval,
that Suffield winter,
look like to you?

This plush little bit
of history, these yellow bones
set, this morning,

against the backdrop
of a CBC radio documentary
on beheadings.

This monkey's skull
is the diameter
of an elaborate

men's wristwatch:
dial-less eyes, one of time's
teeth missing.

It's like a horror-of-war
film, except here
someone has stopped to pen

a set of numbers
in fine black ink
above his eye socket.

His body
flayed clean
down to his hands—

to two cuffs
of copper fur,
like those worn

by kings.

Forget what you've heard
about the fox—her mythic
tricks, her wile, the fabled
sour grapes in Phaedrus.
Forget the story that says
she's a sly ghost
unzipping her skin,
to slip into a blue kimono,
become your mistress.
Place her on the long
metal table in the lab
and empty her out
of our puerile anxieties.
Stroke her fur—
burnishing and near-biblical
in its beauty.

Now touch her dark-tipped ears.
The black caverns of nostril
that could track every hare
in the warren.
Unstuff the tufts of cotton
from where her eyes used to be,
unreel the black dots
someone's drawn on them
in marker.
Whisper the fields back
into her body, like a wish
blown into a dandelion,
and then run with her—
phantom-ride the meadow,
its secret thoroughfares,
arcades of squirrel and vole.

Oh sweet architect of this
imagined world—did you dream
this waft of creek, slope of granite,
the blue palaces of sweet pea?
Let's lift our ears and pretend
the sound of the beetles
working in the bone room
is only a chorus of crickets.
Let's for one second,
    be twinned—
you, the wild animal
slinking along the road,
and me, the girl in the
back window of a car, still
carrying that memory
these ten thousand miles.

Night robber, sleep-taker, acolyte of the moon,
what noise you brought us!
What joyful percussions—
drum of bin lids, cat food tins
rattling in the recycle.
What sly hands you have—how artisanal.

Who caught you, I wonder.
Who brought you here to this mausoleum—
promoted you to *sample of the species,*
called you 'common'—
curled your black paws into boxing gloves
as if you went out fighting.

Here, a nick on your ear,
convict tail laid out behind you;
splay of uneven whiskers.
A blank stare like those found
in mug shots taken at 2AM
in the bleary light of a city station.

Here, a scar on your left wrist
that looks like a bracelet,
a cowlick, small as a fingerprint,
below your chin. And in the fine white fur
of your belly, the teats where you
nursed your young.

To place you back inside the body and back
into the whisking fields—

to reel time, add tissue, tendons, muscles, eyes.
Add the first fall of snow on your smoke-coloured coat.

To flinch and feel flinching move across the skin
like waves radiating from a centre—

to *have* a centre, to register the drop of a thought
echoing down the orbital well.

Or, to embrace absence—the white humps
of the trees hunkering under winter's drop cloth—

a season that challenges the hope
that life trumps death

when everywhere
the latter outweighs us.

So we are fleeting—are the gusts of wind that precede
the absence of weather.

Are, like your skull, both something and nothing—
a *Once-upon-a time*

an *Out in the woods, a half-hour from the village,
a girl in a red cap*—

are, yes, exactly that: a spot of red,
blood in the snow,

animals ourselves.

There will be a soon we cannot imagine
and words sought for that new colour—

songs that slip out of our heads,
plants we nurture that do not flower.

The sky will turn out its pockets like a street thug,
display its empty hands.

We will walk more miles than we thought possible
to kiss a lip of water.

The news will come in swarms,
the broadcasters grown tired.

We will stand in gutted fields stung by
the unholy quiet,

stop speaking of golden things:
sunshine, loosestrife, rows of wheat, corn.

Words become locked boxes we push
under our beds, store in gun cabinets.

Our laughter as canned as the reruns
pirated through satellite stations.

How easily we were once amused!
Duck Dynasty, 19 Kids and Counting—

the nature show where a man sticks his hand
down the throat of a crocodile and pulls out a radio.

The bees will have seen it coming,
our own fading signal—the distant

and zigzagging static
of our extinction—

       now in front of us,
       now behind.

↓ *Anna K— in Newfoundland*

She studies. Imagines her Elsewheres.

This is how they train you:
a Classical education beginning with
Russian history and literature;
forays back to the Greeks.

And music: Mussorgsky and Rimsky-Korsakov.
Hours stationed at the piano
wondering what adornments will complement
her new blue dress.

The natural sciences, which translate
for Anna into afternoons sketching
azaleas to get the pistil,
stamens and petals correct.

At fourteen she begins to think
in English—because there is a push
to be versed this way. *The world, the world,
the world,* her tutor says,

spinning the library globe
with his ungloved finger
so that it whirls and blurs against the novels
she hopes to enter.

The custom, in Russia, is to keep
a mirror under your pillow
in order to dream of the beloved
you'll one day meet,

but Anna folds a map there—
the earth's four corners,
its unfathomable monsters, churning
under the sea of her sleep.

There is a map of the world
with Newfoundland at its centre—

stand on the peninsula,
or a boat trolling out of Bonavista

and the sky organizes itself
accordingly.

Every avenue under the stars
a rocky way of knowing.

So let's gather these netted skirts
and what's known of history—

how slippery it is, how unpredictable,
like those sea creatures

fished from the imagination,
weft into dreams.

How sometimes a stranger appears,
breaks with custom,

comes to study the tongue
of what *belonging* means.

This is the place
Anna's been thinking about:

the one marked in red and pulsing
like a lighthouse beacon.

And so it's here she finds herself:
salt water, salt box house,

streets that slope the hill,
near-Russian winters.

Windowless hours
spent wandering the outports.

A woman wanting
this exact Anywhere;

a Vronsky who could
be anyone.

A man walks into a bar.
No, a woman walks out of one.
Short-skirt, black-boots,

three men around the bottom step,
the press of their eyes following her
as she lightly mounts the stairs.

Later he'll say *I felt you coming*
before you arrived,
if you know what I mean.

The salt hill by the harbour
covered in tarps and tractor tires—
the start of the slippery season.

Here's how it breaks down—
that watery feeling that will make Anna
want to drop to her knees:

harm through action is worse
than harm by omission, and harm intended
is worse than harm unseen.

Harm caused by contact is worse
than harm caused by thought.

As if there's no power
in that last thing.

It's autumn when they meet—
    a block up from the harbour.

Trash bags on the sidewalks
    weighed down with fishing nets,

archways over the stairs
    that mount the hillside.

    A cloud-scuffed sky.

Later, she'll forget who introduced them,
    though she'll remember

the bird spikes lining the stone ledge
    above his head.

This is how it begins: he leans her up
    against a lamppost, recites a poem—

and she lets the words carry her
    toward him.

That night, in bed in her room on Battery Road
    she'll dream a terrible storm—

the fist of the sky
    slamming the water.

This is the violence she's thinking about: the want
    to crack open someone's head,

    drink their thoughts.

He's not the centre of himself, nor the one thing the tour guide
      recommends in the city.

Think of those abandoned villages so remote they only register
      in the If-you-have-four-weeks itinerary:
closed factories, collapsed fishing sheds, shuttered church, wooden slipways.

A desire, in Anna, to get lost there just the same, inscribe herself in his terrain;
      take the hard complexity he is and reduce him to a postcard.

That he has a form, a history, a body—
      is not a man posing for a painting, but what gets found
in the back room of the abandoned butcher's house:

rusty knives, meat hooks, a cutting block—
      the sharp-edged assertion of a wound.

Elsewhere, there are promises made:
a husband, a child, waiting.
Mail that's set on Anna's mahogany desk,
rooms she still calls *home*.

They receive on Mondays
and her son, flaxen-haired and shy,
stands well away from the door
because he does not trust strangers.

Her husband's study a snarl
of committee work: reports and briefs,
dismissals, official stamps to keep
the city in order.

What she misses most about the house
is their large unshuttered library,
its blue velvet chaise; the Faustian
danger of books.

Once, under the linden with her
little boy, she conjured possible futures:
London or Paris, theatres and museums,
the moon tipping its hat to the Seine.

This duplicity one
that's difficult to reside in—
what it means to live with the person
you have yet to become.

Soon, the bronze clock back at home
will strike the hour for dinner.
If Anna presses her ear to Vronsky's chest
she can almost hear it ticking.

The men come in off the boats or they don't.
Mornings she walks the harbour and sees them
standing at their posts, signs on the gangway
stating what time shore leave ends.
He has had many lovers. Has also done his time
on the water, hauling in nets and dropping ropes.
A world of pulleys and railings.

Things he hasn't told her: what he did last week,
where he was last night, how to cut the tongue
from a cod's mouth so it will keep
the violence a secret.
He hasn't touched her like that—
guilt is also conversation, a way of leaning into
another's brutality.

She asks how big cod can get and he gestures
to the table between them.
She's not making more of this than it deserves.
Knows that if she stays long enough the weight
of what he hauls up will seem less and less miraculous.
A plainness akin to any kind of labour —
the act of gutting what sustains us.

In Rome the slaves put clay pots out
on the coldest nights in winter,
leaving water to freeze under
the swollen eye of the moon.

A time of violence.
Ice, an opulence in that dark season.
Each water bearer's body
racked in plank and rope

the long walk from the stream
to the temple
measured
in clouds of breath.

How lucky Anna and Vronsky
are now, in their unflayed season:
a clear road up Signal Hill,
flask of rye, Thermos of tea,

the night sky beaded.
Frost that makes the branches
beautiful, before it makes
them weep.

The raven on the telephone wire
not an auger after all—
just a ragged bird dressed like
a Petersburg gentleman—

clucking his tongue
when Anna walks by.

The going into.
        Entering his house, walking across the room.

Thinking of that closeness: *This is the worst thing that will happen.*
        Saying it.

Then the kiss, an acquiescence that reorders the map,
        that shifts a dark forest to its centre.

Night-time in all directions.

And so, the secret pleasure of rutted roads; how they remind her
        she is travelling.

Nothing here she would slice out of her days,
        out of the newly combed hours.

His fingers in her hair, his hand on her hip, so that time
        unbuckles itself, begins unspooling.

Anna writing down everything that happens
        in that buzzing season—

how golden and unexpected it is— like honey left in the woods
        by a swarm of wild bees.

Hours dropped into her lap, days she lifts to her mouth,
        her tongue touching their sweetness.

Anna wants to say something true
        but her voice is threaded wrong.

A mouth full of zippers,
        a disfiguring disgrace.

What makes the train tracks she is walking on *beautiful*—
        all that progressive symmetry.

Her voice breaking because it cannot make itself up,
        because it is reciting the Unmaking.

The trees stripped bare, the scarf slid off,
        that traitorous unwinding.

As if a thousand maps were cut into pieces,
        and reassembled by a child:

Petersburg rising out of the Bay, Moscow's rivers
        running into a house on Lime Street.

Scale and time, wobbled.

Broken, because even Anna doesn't know
        what will happen—

how one dark freight of thought might come
        to touch another.

That she can touch the map he's drawn on his body—
dig her nail into the black ink of his town:
the metal sheds the moon catches,
and the fish factory, speckled with the blood
the needle spurred as it stitched him
back into the place he came from.

The white-sided house, wharf and cutting tables
raised for a week on the side of his arm.
A small welt set against the fact that in the years after
his mother gave birth to him, she willed him gone.
Look: under Anna's tongue—
the room he was born in.

She's not even in the door and
    her son's throwing a tantrum,
asking *What did you bring me?*

Her husband's hat on the hook,
    head angled over his papers,
dust settling on top of dust.

How was your journey? he finally asks,
    studying her impassive face,
and Anna thinks of the clacking pistons

of the train that brought her here—
    how time seems to have cast her
backwards:

some awful plot that calls for
    lantern light, claw foot tables,
porcelain basins;

imperfect affinities she can
    barely bring herself
to move around.

Days spent drifting through rooms
    trying to imagine what power
might propel her forward—

God of the sealed envelope
    propped up against
the milk jug.

As if a painting hung in a parlour: a family picnic.
Tall black boots on the men, the wife-with-parasol,
a little boy in white gloves. A sky that may have been
sunlit when painted but which has turned over the centuries
into fawn; tufted clouds flocked in the corner of the canvas.
In the foreground a deerhound with perked ears.
Everyone leaning in one direction.

There is no gathering storm here, no sound of approaching
horses. The men are not hunting, do not even
carry guns. The partridges in the distant fields
bask on meadowed terraces.

Is it the first trace of fall that catches her eye?
How autumn makes everything golden.
Anna observing it and the rest of the family following her gaze.
The ash tree leaves hanging like pendelled chandeliers
in a toile room. One pastoral cast against its ornate other.
Each leaf in curtsey to the breeze, waiting
for what might make it sail, for what might spin it
into the one thing it did not know it could become.

Her neighbours finger the sleeves of family life
as if it were a well-made coat.

And yes, she has a decent husband, a marvelling child,
an abacus that clicks bead after bead into place.

So what of honesty? Of what's announced
and what gets pared away?

Even the Egyptians weighed the heart against
enumerations of innocence:

*I have not mistreated cattle, I have not robbed the poor
or held back water in its season.*

Rules of etiquette Anna finds
in *The Book of the Dead.*

*I have not caught fish in their ponds,
I have not snared birds in the reeds of the gods,*

I have not sinned in the Place of Truth.

And once, at least, I stood there.

The two of them on the platform of the station
trying to pin language down: *You'll change me /*
you'll destroy me / I never want to see you again.

Her voice broken. Hanging like strips of bark
after a fire that crossed a hundred acres
to exhaust itself at the start of the bristling fields.

As if the world could fold over itself, deposit
whole cities into the pockets of towns, pour
burning deserts into oceans.

Here, the arrival—how she'll step off the train
of her uncertainties, her failings
a black scarf unfurling behind her.

Every street light, corner grocer—a sureness.
As is the Room's black bear staring into the fluorescence,
the mangy dog who drifts, day after day, past the park.

Though it's early yet—the bed sheets
that usually gust on Gower Street gone for the season;
the blue paint Anna loved, being stripped from its house.

Halfway down Duckworth she asks him
for a proper conversation, and he says,
There are no proper conversations with me.

So they split a glass skull of vodka
from the Queen Street liquor store,
watch the ships being iced into the harbour

with no sign of a breaker to set them free.

There are no trains on this island,
only abandoned stations Anna frequents.

Trains hold a certain nostalgia for her—
like epic Russian novels:

long enough and noisy enough
to carry all her grief.

This winter'd city an outport of ice
slammed into the ocean.

Every mark on his body like that—
ink-dark, bucked and scarred,

then washed over
and made clean.

The two of them standing together
at the lip of the country

long enough to see
what makes them ugly.

Nights so dark they can't tell
the harbour from the narrows,

or the gaping headlands
from the sea.

A constant shrugging off.
Even his posture says *This will come to nothing*.

Still, mid-week, he drives her up to his cottage,
blares the radio.

Spear grass freezing along his property line,
'No Trespassing' signs clanking against the fences.

Three locks on his door. Inside: buckets,
the smell of wood smoke.

Up the hill past the house, seabirds
shucking their meager lunches on the rocks—

one of them dropping a shell
as perfectly coiled as a piece of jewellery.

Anna's studying it when Vronsky comes back
from pitching stones into the cove—

going down on his knees
to press his face into her skirt.

You can inhabit that too: the hollow.
How it curls like a question mark.

Yes—Anna says, *yes*—
ask me for anything.

The hour clangs and he leaves, slamming her front door behind him.
And so Anna scrawls 'unhinged' in the book she's reading.

A novel in which the art of carrying a pitcher of water
often goes unnoticed because it's only a skill of the Help.

This morning delivering two cups of tea up to their room
she'd watched as they'd rocked back and forth on their saucers.

Yes, there are days when her very Self —the Anna she is
when no one's watching—vibrates from want.

Was it only yesterday she'd held the globe of Vronsky's head
as he slept on her lap, imagined their children?

This, she supposes, is her grief—
that men should make her mean—

that they should shape her so unwittingly.

This is the difficulty with endings—
how to proceed from the well of feeling,

and how to sense the size of the well.
How deep, if full or empty,

and if full
to ask whose tears have filled it,

and if empty
if someone has dropped knives there,

and if knives
how they sit—

bared like teeth
in the moonlight

or hidden and waiting
to slice a hand or a foot.

This is the beauty of all that awful
crying—what it whets her against

how it affirms a duty to that most
primal thing: breath. Survival.

He cannot love her, and that absence
of love is a vacancy.

Anna knows it's not this way for everyone.
For some the shape absence takes—

the wet plum bruise of it,
is a flower

and if a flower, something flourishing—
the purled heart

of a chrysanthemum,
the gutted, yielding rose.

This is nothing new. Anna can open
any book in her library and find

love and mourning
in equal measure—

hymns stitched with ragged breathing,
dark cloaks slick as oil.

Easy to mourn death, to raise the bucket
of the body from the ground—

less so to grasp what's gone
and *live*.

In the beginning there was
a well,

and time and space
swept into it

a map of yes, a map
of feeling,

of what latitudes
a heart can contain

if one agrees
to everything.

↓ *Esk*

I.

We arrive at the estate over the course of a day,
gather in the sitting room outside the second library.

*It is said that
'Being' is the
most universal
and the empti-
est of concepts.*

INT. I.51

How strange new faces are: their planes and steeps,
the fixedness of their expression.

The six of us monkish at the start—
spending time alone in silence.

Me, I like the view from the Scottish library best:
green rustling woods, peregrine falcons,

the stoop and flicker of the Esk
shushing below us.

This castle a place of eclipsed views,
of tried and failed investigations.

I'm reading Heidegger here—making notes in light
spalled through quarrelled windows.

My own sense of self dog-eared—
a page I go back to repeatedly:

You give too much / you've not given enough,
though I'm uncertain who's to say.

The best days will be those when I take
the deer-path along the river,

study what the Esk
gives over to its banks:

pottery shards and golf balls,
a bullet casing, the shell of a speckled egg.

The neck of the Esk turning back on itself
like a question—

How much to keep? it asks, and how to measure
the tenor, the pure sound and colour

of what gets carried away.

II.

The world is green this morning—
lit up by spooling leaves and the trees'
various removes and settings.

A protected world: wrought-iron gate
at the top of the roadway, pass code,
stone fences that spike the fields.

Land of teeth, of what crops up
unexpected—a rusty cage
meant for an animal; the myth of a fox.

Me? I'm a novice Buddhist
practising attention—the absent fox
held in my thoughts from a desire to see her.

Everywhere this caginess: the twitchy woods,
nests in the shrugging beech,
birds trying to distract us from their brood.

Later, in the exquisite dullness
of a long afternoon, two hikers
will pass into view below me—

a man in Gor-Tex, a woman with a rucksack,
a wide-eyed stuffed animal
swinging from its strap.

Who sent you? I'll wonder,
as they move between the curtains
of the midsummer trees.

A desire in me to call out to them—
to tell them that the path along the river
circles back on itself

though you can wade across
the rushing Esk, if
you're willing to risk it.

III.

Begin with what presents itself:
a holt of trees, a crumbling turret,
steel girders, moss cladding, the problem
of saying 'castle' in the modern world.
And Rilke in his tower in Trieste,
studying how even a plain button
slips out of its eyelet.

Being-in-the-world shall first be made visible with regard to that item of its structure which is the 'world' itself.

I.III §14

In the village: row houses, a school, a football field.
A cemetery with headstones like those
distance markers placed between settlements
on early Roman roads.
Then: tufts of blond dog hair bedded down
in the verge—a palm-sized mat
the same milk-white as our own dead dog's fur.

Soon, the locals will wander back from work,
Tescos, the pub, the Spar—past signs
that show them how far they've travelled.
And I'll go in, tired of the flickering channels
of weather: bright, then grey, then a pass of rain,
then suddenly verdant again.

One of the ways we know we're here
is because hurt is sometimes electric.
Today was simple: towers of bird song,
intermittent mosquito swarm;
the clutch of fur and flowers I carried with me.

IV.

*And how is
it possible to
'ascertain'
what is
missing...?*

II.IV ⸻ 69

The dead are gone.

Will not burst out of some other-where,
come flying, reveal themselves.

Again, I'm at the window.
This morning: swallows.

And stone, mortar, wall, me.
The invisible hands of the builders—

ghosts already swimming
in the green of this poem's grass.

Who stands to greet you
when the word *dead*

raises its mossy head
from the ground?

It's the wood pigeons who startle me most.
Have you seen them?

Blasting out of thickets
all furious wing-flap and choler.

Tomorrow I'll take the trail
in a new direction.

The dogs will bark from their side of the wall
long before I see them.

Kennel? Shelter?
Abattoir?

Who can say from the peaked roofs
of their patch-wood pens, the barbed wire?

Each morning I'm asked
what I'd like for lunch,

and a woman leaves it
outside my room in a basket.

I can't imagine a day when I won't
consume it all—

when there'd be a scrap left
for anyone.

v.

The starry heads of the woodruff
are saying *No* to the wind,

though they might also be nodding along
to the song of their own great ideas.

Still, today it feels like
the clock of the world,

its ticking heart,
is less fired-up than usual.

The talk last night was of violence,
and the right to be offended.

Tonight I'll aim for lightness
and fail—

forget the names
of the field flowers,

say the wrong things at dinner,
ghost past the dusky mirror.

I'll try talk about the girl I met
at a workshop in London,

the one whose brother
mounted neon signs

on the outside walls
of cemeteries—

*And here too
Dasein's Being
is an issue for
it in a definite
way; and Dasein
comports itself
towards it in the
mode of average
everydayness,
even if this is
only the mode
of fleeing in the
face of it and
forgetfulness
thereof.*

I.I § 9

YOU ARE STILL ALIVE one said,
in a pulsing red fluorescence.

YOU ARE STILL
ALIVE.

VI.

In the woods the rain
types essays on the leaves.

The footpath slick with mud
and dangerous.

This is a protected valley—
if you don't count the chiselled graffiti

and the white blooms of toilet paper
I mistook, at a distance, for flowers.

The rain writing today about
the charred circle of a campfire,

the explosion of bird feathers
hanging in the canopy.

We are getting to know
each other quickly—

a childhood illness, a brother in Iraq,
the strain of coming to terms with

another human being
whose world is hidden from you.

This evening when I mention
the sheer drop to the Esk

in the context of my suicidal tendencies,
it will not go well.

It's too much skin for some—
like the girl whose shirt lifts to reveal

a burn mark,
in the middle of a party.

VII.

After a
theme for
investigation
has been initial-
ly outlined in
positive terms,
it is always im-
portant to show
what is to be
ruled out....

I.I § 10

The winter will not come while we're here. The cold will not
cauterize vines, thump through radiators, rupture pipes.

The power will not fail, stubs of candles be scrounged for
in the backs of empty drawers.

We'll become accustomed to silence though we won't
agree on how it sounds, or the weight of it:

heavy as wet wool or light as the collars of fur
worn by rabbits as they dart from their burrows.

We won't become for each other
the person we'd most like to be.

Such steadiness, such dedication,
impossible.

In a few weeks when the summer rain stops
and the Esk invites us to wade in,

we'll wander the river in T-shirts and shorts
looking for things we won't find:

pottery shards, pewter cups,
a bronze statue saluting us through silt.

Even the yellow Frisbee lost by the farmer's dog
will evade us.

We'll think we know each other well by then,
and be wrong about it,

our legs pushing through the water—
the hope of some bright thing waving under it.

VIII.

Rain gone sideways. Indefinite thunder.

All morning my body leaning
toward the word 'storm'—

I open my window twice
wanting to be sure of it.

1.I 5 9   I am thinking, again, in this rarified air,

of the friend at the bar who said
You are fascinating to yourself.

As if there's some fault in that inventory,
as if it pales against service to another.

It will turn out to be airplanes—engine noise,

a runway out of Edinburgh,
for those flocking south.

I count their hard-winged shapes for half a day,
then turn back to the circling birds,

the lost thing they're hovering over.

One day, my love, I'll be gone—
and you will think *This was her hair,*

*this was her mouth, this was the body
she lived in.*

Tonight I will speak of you at dinner:

my usual orbit of praise
and admiration.

They will start throwing napkins at me,
rolling their eyes, soon.

IX.

The basic state of sight shows itself in a peculiar tendency-of-Being which belongs to everydayness — the tendency towards 'seeing'. We designate this tendency by the term "curiosity" [Neugier], which characteristically is not confined to seeing, but expresses the tendency towards a peculiar way of letting the world be encountered by us in perception.

I.V ⁋ 36

After the war, the artist started
to paint his subjects upside down.

In one work, two huntsmen
saddled on horses

dangle from a snowy field
as if nothing unusual is happening—

as if they weren't pegged
to winter's twig-strewn ceiling

by eight black hooves.

The furniture in my room
is over one-hundred years old—

embroidered with deer and the
hounds who hunt them.

The fabric on the chair
I'm sitting on, torn—

strands of the horsehair
it's stuffed with

knit into the rug.

This must be why I sometimes dream
of meadows carpeted above—

and that I've run a thousand miles
to dip my head

into the poppled sky
of the Esk.

Can you see how exhausted
this makes me?

This trough of stars in my mouth.

X.

*Does not dying
mean going-out-
of-the-world,
and losing one's
Being-in-the
world? Yet when
someone has
died, his Being-
no-longer-in-
the-world (if we
understand it
in an extreme
way) is still a
Being....*
II.1547

This morning the field
is lit with birds

whose migrations
are a mystery.

Their forms rising and falling
in the birch stand

while I think about
my mentor's death

and struggle to name
what surrounds me:

starlings, finches, waxwings,
a blackbird.

The sound of the wind
rushing the Esk,

like the gust of cars
on a motorway.

Months from now I'll hear
a young poet read

and he'll brag that his book
doesn't have a bird in it anywhere.

Fair enough, I suppose—
though I wonder

what else circles death
so diligently?

That dark wing
sweeping over me.

XI.

The 'deceased'
[Der "Ver-
storbene"] as
distinct from
the dead person
[dem Gestor-
benen], has
been torn away
from those who
have 'remained
behind'.... The
deceased has
abandoned our
'world'.... But
in terms of that
world [Aus ihr
her] *those who*
remain can still
be with him.

II.I § 47

One morning over breakfast I confess
that I'm more afraid of being dead
          than I am of dying.

I seem to be in the minority in this.
We are a table of atheists—
          and so first there is

the problem of logic:
of how, dead, we come to know
          we're nothing.

This, over porridge served in pewter bowls
engraved with the names of the ships
          they were made for.

Today I have HMS Hope,
though tomorrow it could be HMS Essex
          or Courageous.

All of us thinking through the slack
mouth of death into what it means
          to be dead and know it.

To watch a stranger
scrape the bottom of a bowl
          you once met with a spoon.

XII.

And now, the problem of letting go.
How some nights I feel like an amateur

pulling a length of scarves
from my throat.

And sometimes anger and spite,
which I wear like rain.

The girl beside me on the night bus
from Edinburgh—in her new blue top,

jeans and Docs—bites her nails,
gnaws her thumb.

I get off at the stop near the top gate
and she drags her moon face behind me.

Let's agree that losing love
is sometimes a violence.

Like that bit in the second act
where the magician says

Now watch me saw
this woman in half.

Maybe we're all charismatics—
want a tent flap to push through

a gift for prophecy,
like-minded congregations.

Dasein exists
as an entity
for which, in
its Being,
that Being is
itself an issue.
Essentially
ahead of itself,
it has projected
itself upon its
potentiality-
for-Being.... In
its projection
it reveals itself
as something
which has been
thrown.

II.VI § 79

Tonight in my room
I'll sit at this desk, send out

my hopeful missives. The Esk
battering her banks below.

Yes, there are days when I think
I can see what's coming

but then the light
shifts.

XIII.

In my last week I become
detached, caught up

in being and not being,
unsure of the distance

between self and others—
our quick and shifting allegiances

that slipped sense of having
said too much to some.

An urgency, for a few of us,
with our writing—

while the others seem to spend
whole days lounging

in overstuffed chairs and soft beds
reading Knausgård.

I'm left out of this, willfully—
discover instead a stillness

in a thicket where deer
bed down by the Esk.

The long grass folded over
like page corners

and the hours of the deers' absence
unrushed and easily readable,

*And to what
is one called
when one is
thus appealed
to? To one's
own Self. Not
to what Dasein
counts for, can
do, or concerns
itself with in
being with
one another
publicly, nor
to what it has
taken hold of,
set about, or let
itself be carried
along with.*

II.II ∫ 56

though on my last morning
I'll swear I can feel

a lingering warmth
under the palm of my hand.

XIV.

I would have liked to have
left as friends, to feel
some sort of new tethering.
A shade more certainty
than I felt going in.

Even Heidegger has disappointed:
he's wrong about animals, and sometimes
when he's right about Being,
he's shining his flashlight so far down
the wavering Esk I can't see it.

A year from now, driving an Island road
with my high beams on
after a panel discussion
on 'the writer as subject'
a deer will leap out in front of me—

arc of white fur over her snout,
black tail twitching.
She'll stop in the middle of the road
and we'll stay twenty feet apart
for a full minute—

my rearview mirror dark,
dashboard lit blue,
the deer's ears turning like satellites
toward the sound
of Bon Iver on my stereo.

Truth is, there seems to be an ease
with which I let people go.
I'll have done it again recently—

*When one
takes one's
ontological ori-
entation from
something that
is constantly
present-at-
hand, one
either looks for
the problem of
the Continuity
of time or
leaves this
impasse alone.*

II.VI ⸱ 81

with all the deleting and
unfollowing that now entails.

The deer will be done with me
before I'm done with her,
will step lightly toward the woods,
pause briefly at the ditch,
look back at the car.

I will be stupidly grateful for this—
how some good-byes get *said*,
how the last light glinting
off a river
can stay with you.

Flicker.
      Swish.

One minute she was standing there,
the next minute gone.

And how effortless

      the lift.

A number of these poems have appeared in literary magazines. I'm grateful to the editors of *The Fiddlehead, Prism International, The Malahat Review, Room Magazine, Riddle Fence* and *Best Canadian Poetry* (2013) for their support. ¶ The title 'On The Melancholy of a World Eternally Under Construction' is a line from Bohumil Hrabal's novel *Too Loud a Solitude*. ¶ The poems in 'I Came To See the Beautiful Things' were written during a residency at the Beaty Biodiversity Museum in Vancouver, BC. I'm grateful to Dr. Rick Taylor, Mairin Kerr and Chris Stinson for their time and their willingness to let me handle the specimens in their collection. The title of the series comes (loosely) from Susan Sontag's essay 'Unguided Tour'. ¶ 'Anna K— in Newfoundland' was first drafted during a residency at Memorial University in St. John's, Newfoundland. Thank you to the Canada Council for funding the residency and to the English Department for their hospitality. A number of the titles in 'Anna K— in Newfoundland' were inspired by lines in Leo Tolstoy's *Anna Karenina*. The first line in 'And Then She Thought ...' is a modified version of a first line by Jan Zwicky. ¶ Much of 'Esk' was written during a residency at Hawthornden Castle in Scotland. Thank you to my fellow writers, the administrators and house staff, and to Dr. Simon Malpas who had me wrestling Heidegger that summer. The offset quotes in this series come from the Macquarrie and Robinson translation of Martin Heidegger's *Being and Time*. ¶ 'the floor: wood plank ...' in 'oh, heart—' is for Rob and Zuse. ¶ 'Hummingbirds, Unlabelled' is for Elise Partridge. ¶ 'Esk X' is for Dermot Healy. ¶ The Dermot Healy quote at the start of the book comes by kind permission from the Estate of Dermot Healy (The Gallery Press, Loughcrew, Oldcastle, County Meath, Ireland). The lines are from 'The Quick Slow Boat' in *The Travels of Sorrow* (2015). ¶ It's a gift to have good readers to nudge one's work along. I'm especially grateful to Miranda Pearson, and to Nelia Botelho, and Anne Simpson for their insights and suggestions on these poems. Special thanks for various acts of kinship and encouragement go to Kerry Ohana, Claudia Casper, Rob Finley, Joel Thomas Hynes, Rochelle Baker, Patrick Warner, and Jan Zwicky. ¶ I've always admired Gaspereau Press. Thank you, Andrew, for giving this book such a wonderful home. ¶ Most of all: thank you, Glenn. For the ordinary and the extraordinary, this life, our family. 'oh, heart—' is for you.

ABOUT THE TYPE

This book is set in LAURENTIAN, a digital typeface designed by Rod McDonald of Lake Echo, Nova Scotia. Originally envisioned as a compact magazine type for *Maclean's* in 2001, the type soon evolved into an efficient, highly-legible Garamond-flavoured text face suitable for a wide range of uses. Gaspereau Press tested beta versions of the font on its presses before the type was made available to the general trade by Monotype in 2002. The custom version used in this book employs lengthened descenders which I enticed Rod McDonald to create for use in typesetting books. The smattering of Greek found in 'Esk' is set in WILSON, a revival of Alexander Wilson's eighteenth-century Glaswegian Greek types revived in digital form by Matthew Carter in the 1990s. AS

7   6   5   4   3   2   1

Library & Archives Canada Cataloguing in Publication

Hunter, Aislinn, 1969–, author
    Linger, still / Aislinn Hunter.

Poems.
ISBN 978-1-55447-170-6 (softcover)

    I. Title.

PS8565.U5766L56 2017   C811'.6   C2017-901257-6

GASPEREAU PRESS LIMITED * GARY DUNFIELD
& ANDREW STEEVES * PRINTERS & PUBLISHERS
47 Church Avenue, Kentville, Nova Scotia B4N 2M7
Literary Outfitters & Cultural Wilderness Guides

Canada   NOVA SCOTIA